Coding with Python

A Simple Guide to Start learning:

Lots of Exercises and Projects for

Distributed Computing Systems

TIM WIRED

Table of Contents

Introduction 1

Chapter 1: The Python Language 5

    What is the Python Language? 6

    The Benefits of Python 9

    The Python Interpreter 14

Chapter 2: How to Install Python On Your Computer
.... 17

    Installing Python 19

        Python – V 19

        Python3 – V 20

Chapter 3: The Important Basics to Writing Any Code
in Python 25

    The Python Keywords 25

    How to Write a Comment 26

    The Importance of the Variables 27

    Why Focus on the Classes? 27

    Naming Your Identifiers 28

    A Look at the Operators 29

Chapter 4: Python As An OOP Language and How to
Start Writing Your Own Classes 31

    Some of the Features of OOP Languages 35

    Coding Your Own Classes 38

Chapter 5: Working with the Python Namespaces ... 47

    What are These Namespaces? 49

What is the Scope? 50

Chapter 6: The Decision Control Statements...........53

Decision Control Statement # 1: The If Statement............ 54

Decision Control Statement # 2: The If Else Statement..... 56

Decision Control Statement # 3: The Elif Statement 59

Chapter 7: How to Handle and Raise Your Own Exceptions 63

Raising an Exception.. 66

How Can I Define My Own Exceptions? 68

Chapter 8: Inheritances and How They Can Help You Reuse Code and Save Time 73

Overriding the Base Class.. 76

Chapter 9: Creating Your Own Loops in Python.......79

The While Loop 82

The For Loop.. 83

The Nested Loop 86

Chapter 10: The Python Variables 89

Assigning a Value to the Variable 91

Chapter 11: Understanding the Operators and Where They Come Into Play 97

The Arithmetic Operators.. 98

The Comparison Operators 98

The Logical Operators 100

The Assignment Operators 101

Chapter 12: Working with Regular Expressions 103

Some of the Basic Patterns to Use 105

How to Do a Query 107

Using the Search Method 108

Using the Match Method 109

Using the Findall Method...................................109

Chapter 13: The Files of Python 111

How to Create Your Own Files 113

Handling the Binary Files.................................. 116

Opening a New File 117

Seeking a File 119

Chapter 14: Tips and Tricks to Learn More About Python..121

Do a Little Coding at a Time............................. 122

Do Some of the Practice Options 124

Print Out Things Along the Way........................126

Comment Out Your Code 127

Practice Makes Perfect 128

Ask for Help When Needed 129

Learn Some Common Error Messages 131

Don't Be Scared to Try Something New............132

Print Off Some Cheat Sheets 134

Conclusion 137

Description 141

Introduction

Congratulations on purchasing *Coding with Python,* and thank you for doing so.

The following chapters will discuss all of the different parts that we need to know when we are ready to start coding in Python and seeing some of the results that we want as a beginner with our own codes. There may be some other options out there that you are able to choose when it comes to writing out codes and getting your programs and applications done, but you will quickly see that none of them are going to provide you with the options and the versatility that you are looking for like we can see with the Python coding language.

Inside this guidebook, we are going to spend some time looking at the Python language and all that it is able to provide for us when it is time to start our work with coding. You will find that while this is a simple language to work with, it will still provide you with all of the options and more that you are looking for overall. And we are going to explore a lot of these in this guidebook today!

To start with, we are going to spend some time taking a look at the basics of the Python language. We will find that we can learn about the benefits of this language, why you would want to work with this language, and so much more. Then we are going to move on to some of the basics that come with downloading and installing the Python language on your system, and some of the most basic parts that come with coding in this kind of language. This will help us to make sure that we are able to get all of the parts done that we are looking for and will ensure that we are able to get the results that we want.

From there, we can then move on to some of the other options of what we are able to do when it comes to the Python language. For example, we are going to find that we are able to work with things like creating our own classes and exploring some of the cool things that we are able to do when it comes to working with an OOP language. This is a really neat feature that comes with some of the more modern coding languages that are out there, and it is really important to helping us to get things done with some of the codings that we want to work with.

There are a lot of other things that we are able to work with when it comes to the Python language, and this guidebook is going to help us walk through this and see all of the really neat things that we are able to do within this kind of language. For example, we will take a look at how to work with the variables, the conditional statements, so the program is able to make some decisions on its own without the programming having to guess what input the user is going to rely on all of the time and more.

This is just the beginning of what we will be able to do with this kind of programming language though. We will also take a look at how we can focus on the loops to help us save some coding space and get the language to repeat the same line more than once. We can look at inheritances to see how we can reuse some of the previous parts of the code that we need to make our codes stronger and better than ever before. And we will even look at how to handle some of the exceptions that may show up in your coding to ensure that you are able to keep things organized and working the way that you would like along the way.

At the end of this guidebook, we are going to take a look at some of the simple tips and tricks that you are able to follow in order to get some of the best results that you would like out of the Python language. As a beginner, getting started on the right track will be able to help you get the most out of your coding needs. And this chapter will make sure that you are set up and ready to go when it is time to work on all of your codes.

All of these points are going to work together to help us to really see some great results when it comes to writing out our own codes. No matter what your goal is when it comes to writing out some of the codes that we need in Python, or for any other language, learning the basics and how we are able to use these for some of our needs are going to be so important. We are going to make sure that we go through these basics and learn some of the parts to help us really get things done in no time.

There may be quite a few coding languages out there that you are able to work with. But it is important for us to spend some time looking at the different parts that come with this coding language so that we are able to write out some of the codes that we want to use at this time as well. When you are ready to learn how to work with the Python coding language and see what this kind of language is able to do for your websites, programs, and applications, then make sure to read this guidebook to help you get started.

There are plenty of books on this subject on the market, thanks again for choosing this one! Every effort was made to ensure it is full of as much useful information as possible; please enjoy it!

Chapter 1: The Python Language

Welcome to the world of Python programming! There are a lot of different options that you are able to choose when it is time to do some of the codings that you would like. But we have to remember that out of all of these, one of the best options that will help you to get some of the coding done that you would like. This guidebook is going to take some time to look at the Python language and what you are able to do with it to get your results in no time at all.

The Python language is one of the easier of the languages to learn, which is good news for someone who is just getting started with coding. But don't let this fool you; it has all of the power, features, and more that you need in order to really push yourself forward and to help you see some amazing results with the coding that you would like to use. Let's take a look at the Python language and what we are able to do when it comes to using this language for all of your coding needs.

What is the Python Language?

In technical terms, you will find that Python is going to be a great coding language that we are able to work with when it is time to handle some of the codings that you would like to get done. This is going to be integrated with some of the dynamic semantics that is going to help with issues of app development and web development. It is going to be a field of Rapid Application Development because it is going to provide us with a way to work with dynamic typing and binding options.

One of the nice things that come with Python is that it is relatively simple, so it will be easy to learn. This is because it is going to require a unique syntax that focuses on readability, so it is easier to use. Developers will be able to translate and read the code of Python much easier than some of the other languages that are out there.

Thanks to this, we will see a reduction in the cost of program maintenance and development because it is going to allow the teams to work in a more collaborative manner, and there will not be any barriers that come with significant language and experiences like other options.

In addition, Python is going to support the use of modules and packages, which is going to mean that programs can be designed in a more modular style, and the code can be reused with more than one project at a time. once you have been able to develop a module or a package that you need, it can be scaled to be used in all of the projects out there, and it is easy to export these modules.

One of the most promising benefits that come with Python is that both the standard library as well as the interpreter are going to be available for us to use for free, in both the source and the binary form, based on what you would like to work with. Here is not going to be any kind of exclusivity either, because Python and all of the necessary tools that are going to be available on all of the major platforms. This means that Python can really be an enticing option to work with for developers who do not want to worry about some of the higher costs that work with development like other options do.

We can then take a look at some of the basics that come with Python. Python is going to be a general-purpose programming language, which is going to be another way to say that we are able to work with nearly everything. Most importantly, it is going to be known as an interpreted language, which means that the code that you are writing out is not going to be translated over to a format that is computer-readable when it is time to run through it.

While most of the languages for programming are going to do this conversion before the program can even run, this is not something that Python is going to work with. This type of language is going to be known as a scripting language because, in the beginning, it was more about helping you to work on some beginner projects. But over time, you will find that it is going to be expandable to some of the other projects that you would like to work with as well.

The concept of these kinds of scripting languages has changed quite a bit since it began. This is because Python is going to be used in a lot of different situations, such as to help us to write out large and commercial style applications rather than just some small and banal ones. This reliance on Python has grown more and more as we see more reliance and use on the internet.

We will also find that a large majority of web applications and a lot of different platforms out there are going to rely on Python, including the search engine of Google, YouTube, and some of the transactions that happen on the New York Stock Exchange that are based online. You know that when a system is able to handle some of these major things, that it is going to be a serious language that is going to help you to get a lot done.

As we can see, there are a lot of different parts that are going to happen when it is time to work with the Python programming language. There are a lot of different parts that come with the Python language, and learning how to make it work for our needs is going to make sure that we are going to be able to write out some of the programs that we would like as well.

The Benefits of Python

There are actually going to be a lot of different benefits that we are able to look at when it is time to handle some of your coding needs with the help of the Python coding language. In fact, this is often one of the most popular coding languages out there because there are so many options that we need to work with and so many benefits that come with this language. For someone who is just starting out and is not sure which kind of coding language to go with, you will find that Python is one of the best options to work with in order to really see some results in no time. Let's take a look at some of the benefits of the Python language, even if you are brand new to the world of coding overall.

To start with, Python is a language that has been designed to help a beginner out with some of their coding needs. If you are not certain about how to get started with some of the coding that you would like, and you want to get started, then Python is going to be one of the best options that you are able to work with overall. It was designed to make coding more accessible to those who have never done any coding in the past, with easy syntax and English as the primary language that comes with this.

If you have been worried about working with the Python language, and you want to ensure that you are actually able to handle some of the codes that you want, whether it is a simple code or a more complicated option, you will find that the Python language is going to be one of the best options to work with overall.

The good news here is that the Python language, even though it has been designed with a beginner in mind, it is still going to be one of the best options for you to use when it comes to power and strength that you need to get things done. You can work with machine learning, data science, and more all with this kind of language, which is going to really help you to see some of the results that you are looking for when it comes to seeing the most out of your own coding, even when you are a beginner.

Along with this same note, you will find that the Python language is going to come with a lot of support libraries to work with, as well. It is not going to take you a lot of time or research to figure out that the Python language has a ton of libraries and extensions that can work along with it. Depending on what you would like to do with some of your coding, you will find that you can get the library or the extension that you need, including with machine learning, math, science, data science, and more.

This is going to provide the beginner with a ton of help when they are first getting started with a language, and it is really going to make things easier when you get to coding. You will be able to also find more functions, classes, objects, and more when you decide to add in some of these parts to the process as well. You can also add in these libraries to make sure that you have the power and the functionality that you need along the way too.

Integration features: Python can be great because it integrates what is known as the Enterprise Application Integration. This really helps with a lot of the different things you want to work on in Python, including COBRA, COM, and more. It also has some powerful control capabilities as it calls directly through Java, C++, and C. Python also has the ability to process XML and other markup languages because it can run all of the modern operating systems, including Windows, Mac OS X, and Linux through the same kind of byte code.

The next benefit that we are going to see is that this language is going to add in some more of the productivity that the programmer gets to enjoy. The Python language is going to have a lot of designs with it that is more object-oriented, and this also allows it to work with a ton of support libraries. Because of these resources, and how easy it is to use the program, it is possible for the programmer to get more done and increase the amount of productivity that they are able to see.

Another great benefit that is going to come with this is that the Python language is going to really have a great community of other coders and developers to work with. Since Python is considered one of the most popular coding languages out there, this means that you are going to find a ton of communities out there that you are able to use to help you get better with programming.

When you work on some of your own codes, you will find that sometimes things are not going to match up the way that you would like, or you end up with some troubleshooting that you just can't figure out. Or maybe you just want to learn something new and need help getting it done. That is where these communities are going to come into play. You can visit these communities to ask questions, to get some help, and even learn something new along the way.

And finally, we are going to take a look at how the Python code is going to be open-sourced. This may not mean all that much right now, but it does mean that we will be able to use the code for free and make the changes and modifications that we need in order to really get our codes to run properly. It also means that you can easily download and use the original Python in any manner that you would like.

Of course, there are some companies that may have taken Python and added some additional features and more to help out with Python. And if you choose to work with some of these, you may need to spend a bit of money to download and use them. But it is completely possible that you can get started with some of the programming that you want to do in Python all for free and without having to worry about having to deal with the copyright.

There are a lot of things to enjoy when it comes to working with the Python language, and we have just gotten started with this list. As you will quickly see through this process, and as we go through some more of the steps that are needed in this guidebook, it is going to be a lot easier to see some more of these benefits as we go through the coding as well.

The Python Interpreter

When we are taking a look at the standard installation that is found with Python, and when we are able to work with the version that is found on www.python.org, you will find that there are a lot of files that are found with this. It is going to contain documentation, the information that you need licensing, and some of the files that you need to develop the codes that you would like. These are going to include the Shell, IDLE, and the interpreter.

The first thing that we are going to spend our time here is the Python interpreter. This is going to be responsible because it is responsible for helping us to execute any of the scripts that we want to write. The interpreter is able to take all of the script files that you write out in this and turns them into instructions. Then it will go through and write them out based on the codes that you would like to work with as well.

While we are here, we also need to take a look at the part that is known as the Python IDLE. This is going to be known as the Integrated Development and Learning Environment. And it is important because it will hold onto all of the other tools that you need to help make developing all of the programs that you want in Python as easy as possible. Depending on which version of Python that you are working with, the IDLE can also be extensive, or it can be a bit easier to work with as well.

If you don't like the version that is on with Python when you download it, there are often other methods and versions that you can choose to download, as well. And at the same time, you are able to find a new text editor to handle some of the work that you are doing. This is something that is important when you want to make sure that you get specific features to help you get your work done, as well. But the traditional form of the IDLE and text editors that come with the original download of Python will really help you to get some of the work done that you would like.

We also have to make sure that we are working with a good Python Shell along the way. This is going to be an interactive command-line driven interface that is going to be found in the interpreter that you work with. This will hold onto some of the commands that you will want to write out. if the shell is able to understand what you are writing out, then it is going to be helpful at going through and executing all of the code that you want to write. But if something goes wrong and it doesn't understand the code, or you are not able to write it out in the proper manner, then you will end up with an error message showing up on the system instead.

All of these different parts are going to be important when you would like to write out some of the codes that you have in Python. When you are working with the installation of this language through the website above, all of these parts are automatically going to be installed on your system for you, and this makes it easy without any additional steps to be taken. But if you decide to go through and get the version of Python that you want to use from another location, check out to see whether these are going to contain everything that you need or not before you try to work with your own coding.

Chapter 2: How to Install Python On Your Computer

Now that we know a bit more about the Python language and what all it is able to do, it is time for us to learn how we are able to install the Python language on our system. The good news here is that this language is going to be able to provide us with a lot of easy steps to get the files we need to be downloaded on any computer that we want, regardless of the operating system that is found there. This means that regardless of whether you are going to work with Windows, Linux, or Mac, you will be able to make this all work and can start using the Python language in no time.

While we are going to take a look at how to get going with the installation process of Python on all three of the major operating systems in a moment, we are going to bring up a few ideas ahead of time. First, we need to make sure that we have an IDE with this, and usually a text editor as well. This will ensure that we are able to actually write the codes. So, no matter where we get the Python file from, we have to make sure that it is going to have the right files so that you can actually write out the codes that you want.

For our purposes here, we are going to spend some time looking at installing the Python language from the website www.python.org. This is the original website that comes with the Python language and will provide you with a free version of Python. You will also be assured that when you download this website, you will then be able to go through and have all of the files that are needed to get started with this all in one place.

Keep in mind when you work with the Python language, and you decide to work with a third-party website to download this, make sure that it has all of the files that you need ahead of time. this will make it easier for you to get started with the coding right after the installation is done. Keep in mind also that when you install some of these third-party versions, they may cost a bit to get started.

With this in mind, let's take a look at some of the steps that you are able to use in order to get the Python language, and all of the files that you need, on any operating system that you would like.

Installing Python

The first operating system that we are going to take a look at is how to install the Python language on a Mac operating system. The good news is that with this operating system, there is usually some version of Python 2 already preinstalled on the system. The exact version of this Python that you would like to work with is going to depend on which version of this operating system that is on your system. If you would like to figure out which one is there, open up your terminal app on the Mac and type in the code below:

Python – V

This is also going to show you some kind of number so that you can see which version of Python is there. you are also able to choose to install the Python 3 on the system if you would like, and it isn't going to be necessary to go through and uninstall this as you go through it, even if you do upload the Python 3 version of your choice. First, we need to make sure that we will not have one of these versions on your computer already or not. The coding that we will be able to use with this one will include:

Python3 – V

The default on OS X is that Python 3 is not going to be installed at all. If you want to use Python 3, you can install it using some of the installers that are on Python.org. This is a good place to go because it will install everything that you need to write and execute your codes with Python. It will have the Python shell, the IDLE development tools, and the interpreter. Unlike what happens with Python 2.X, these tools are installed as a standard application in the Applications folder.

Another option that we are able to spend some time on and work with is going to be the Windows system. This one is going to be a bit different than what we will see with the Mac operating system, but it is still something good that we are able to work with as well. You will find though that this one will not automatically have a version of Python on it at all unless you actually got the computer from someone who did it ahead of time for you.

This is because Microsoft has come up with their own programming language, and this is why we are going to see that the Python language is not going to be present on these systems. The good news is that you can still install Python on your system, and it is going to work just fine for your needs. It just takes a few more steps to get it all done than you would see with some of the other options. The steps that we need to work within order to get the Python language to work on a Windows operating system will include:

To set this up, you need to visit the official Python download page and grab the Windows installer. You can choose to do the latest version of Python 3, or go with another option. By default, the installer is going to provide you with the 32-bit version of Python, but you can choose to switch this to the 64-bit version if you wish. The 32-bit is often best to make sure that there aren't any compatibility issues with the older packages, but you can experiment if you wish.

Now right-click on the installer and select "Run as Administrator." There are going to be two options to choose from. You will want to pick out "Customize Installation"

On the following screen, make sure all of the boxes under "Optional Features" are clicked and then click to move on.

While under Advanced Options" you should pick out the location where you want Python to be installed. Click on Install. Give it some time to finish and then close the installer.

Next, set the PATH variable for the system so that it includes directories that will include packages and other components that you will need later. To do this, use the following instructions:

Open up the Control Panel. Do this by clicking on the taskbar and typing in Control Panel. Click on the icon.

Inside the Control Panel, search for Environment. Then click on Edit the System Environment Variables. From here, you can click on the button for Environment Variables.

Go to the section for User Variables. You can either edit the PATH variable that is there, or you can create one.

If there isn't a variable for PATH on the system, then create one by clicking on New. Make the name for the PATH variable and add it to the directories that you want. Click on close all the control Panel dialogs and move on.

Now you can open up your command prompt. Do this by clicking on Start Menu, then Windows System, and then Command Prompt. Type in "python." This is going to load up the Python interpreter for you.

Don't let all of these steps scare you as you go through this process. It is actually quite a bit easier to work with than it looks, and in no time at all, you will be able to create a program that works well and does what you would like. Once you are done working through the steps above, the Python language will be up and running on your computer, and ready to go for all of your needs, even on the Windows operating system.

And finally, we are going to take a look at some of the steps that you can take in order to get the Python language set up and ready to go on your operating system in no time. The first step that we are going to do with Linux, similar to what we did with the Mac operating system, is to check whether or not Python 3 is found on your system. You are then supposed to open up the command prompt in this operating system and use the code below to help you get started:

```
$ python3 - - version
```

If you are on Ubuntu 16.10 or newer, then it is a simple process to install Python 3.6. you just need to use the following commands:

```
$ sudo apt-get update
$ sudo apt-get install Python3.6
```

If you are relying on an older version of Ubuntu or another version, then you may want to work with the deadsnakes PPA, or another tool, to help you download the Python 3.6 version. The code that you need to do this includes:

```
$ sudo apt-get install software-properties-common
$ sudo add-apt repository ppa:deadsnakes/ppa
# sudo apt-get update
```

```
$ sudo apt-get install python3.6
```

The good news with this is that if you have worked with some of the other distributions of Linux in the past, then you should already have a version of Python 3 installed on your system. If you have not gone through and worked with some of the other distributions of Python before, then you will need to go through and add this onto your computer. You can even go through and install a more recent version of Python on the computer when you need it.

Chapter 3: The Important Basics to Writing Any Code in Python

Before we dive into some of the more complicated codes and methods that we are able to do with the Python language, it is time for us to spend some time learning the basics. These will ensure that we are set up for some of the more complicated options later on, and will ensure that we are going to see the best results later on with our coding. Some of the most important coding basics that we need to know in Python will include:

The Python Keywords

The Python keywords are going to be important because they allow us to take charge and provide some of the commands that we need inside of our code. These are reserved options and words in the language, ones that should only be used in order to tell the compiler the commands that you would like for it to follow. There are quite a few of these that are going to show up in the Python language, but if we are not careful and we don't use it in the proper way, the compiler will get confused and will run an error message for us. Remember what the keywords in Python are, and then just use them in the right place as the commands that you need.

How to Write a Comment

```
#!/usr/bin/env python
""" 

Docstring

"""
# Comment
myvar="String"
```

We can't get too far in our discussion of the basics of Python without taking a look at the comments that are there and what we are able to do with these. If you are writing out some of the codes that you want to use, there are times when you will want to leave a note or a message inside of the code, letting others know what you are doing in the code or why one part is important. But you want to make sure that you are adding these without ruining the code and not getting it to work.

We are able to do all of this with the help of the comments. In Python, we will work with the # symbol to let the compiler know that we want to add in a comment at that point, and then the compiler will know to skip right over that part without concentrating on it or stopping at it at all. This makes it easier to add in as many of these comments as you would like. But it is often best to keep the number of these down to a minimum to help make sure that your code is as nice and organized as possible.

The Importance of the Variables

Variables are another part of the code that you will need to know about because they are so common in your code. The variables are there to help store some of the values that you place in the code, helping them to stay organized and nice. You can easily add in some of the values to the right variable simply by using the equal sign. It is even possible for you to take two values and add them to the same variables if you want, and you will see this occur in a few of the codes that we discuss through this guidebook. Variables are very common, and you will easily see them throughout the examples that we show.

Why Focus on the Classes?

When we work with the Python code, you will quickly find that the classes are going to be important when we are working with our codes. These classes are going to be the basic organizational structure that comes with Python and other OOP languages and will ensure that all of the different items in our codes, or the objects, are going to be organized and will come up when we need them

As we go through this guidebook, you will see that we do spend some time talking about classes and how we are able to organize them to make as much sense as possible. But there are a lot of benefits that come with these classes and being able to make them work for our needs, and creating them in a manner that will hold onto the objects that we have, is going to be very important.

Naming Your Identifiers

Your identifiers can be important to your code as well, and in Python, there are quite a few identifiers to work with too. You will find that they come in at a lot of different names, and you may seem them as functions, entities, variables, and classes. When you are naming an identifier, you can use the same information and the same rules will apply for each of them, which makes it easier for you to remember the rules.

The first rule to remember is when you name these identifiers. You have many options when you are naming your identifiers. For example, you can rely on both uppercase and lowercase letters with naming, as well as any number and the underscore symbol. You can also combine any of these together. One thing to remember here is that you can't start the name with a number, and there shouldn't be any spaces between the words that you write out. So, you can't write out 3words as a name, but you can write out words3 or threewords. Make sure that you don't use one of the keywords that we discussed above or you will end up with an error.

A Look at the Operators

The operators are a simple idea that we are able to work with when it comes to handling stuff in the Python language. These are simple, but they do help to add in some of the focus and power that we need in order to get more done when we are in this language. There are a number o different operators that we are able to focus on in the codes, so you are able to choose the one that is best for your needs.

For example, you can work with the arithmetic operators to help you finish some of the mathematical equations that you would like. You can work with the comparison operators to make sure that it is going to work to compare more than one part of the code together. And we can work with the assignment operators to ensure that we are able to assign the right value to the variable that we need along the way.

These are just a few of the basics that we will need when it is time to work with the Python language and get it up and running. As you go through this guidebook more and more over time, you will see a lot of these basics show up, and then you will feel more confidence over the work that you have been able to do. Make sure to study these a bit more and learn just why they are important to some of the coding that we are going to do here.

Chapter 4: Python As An OOP Language and How to Start Writing Your Own Classes

As we go through and look at some of the things that come with an OOP, or object-oriented programming, languages. Python is considered one of these kinds of languages and will help us to make codes a lot easier to work with. These types of languages will work with classes and objects that are pretty easy to manipulate, as well. These language types are going to work with the idea of classes and objects so that you can keep the code as organized as possible and can help you to get things done.

One of the features that you are going to enjoy when it comes to working with an OOP language is that the procedure that comes with any object that you use is going to come with some power to help access the fields of data, and in some cases, these objects can come in and make some modifications. When we look at an OOP language, you are able to design the program in the manner that you would like, simply by using a series of objects up and then getting them to interact with one another.

This may seem like a simplistic view to take of things, and if you have been a bit worried about doing anything in coding because of some of the challenges that are there, you may feel that taking this approach is going to leave you missing something. Or you may worry that the Python language is not going to have the power that you need to get the work done based on your programming needs.

You will quickly see that the OOP languages are important, and they can really add in a lot of the diversity that is needed for some of your codings. Each language is going to come with some languages, but the ones that you are likely to use, including the Python language, is going to be based on classes. What this means is that the code is going to have each of our objects belong to a class, which can help us to keep things organized, and will give us the freedom to know which objects we will need to work with.

As you work through Python, you will quickly find that an OOP language can make programming and code writing easier. If you ever spent time working with some of the older coding languages, you will notice that those older ones are much harder to work with and that OOP can make things easier. With the older coding languages, it's possible for your objects and other parts of the code to move around or end up in a different location than you had meant, which can make it hard to write the code and even debug it. But with an OOP language, you won't run into this problem because of the way that things are organized.

Before we go further into OOP languages and what they mean, we need to do a quick summary of classes and how they work. Classes are like small containers. You can pick any name that you want for the classes and then add in any item that you would like. Of course, to keep things organized and to help you call up these classes later on in your code, it may be a good idea to pick out a name that describes what is held inside.

When you decide that it is a good idea to work with these various objects that are in the code, you will find that these work the best because they can match up with actual items outside of the program. For example, you can work with an object that is a car, or one that is a book and then a third that is a ball. You also get the option of being able to pick out an object that is a bit more abstract, though this does add in another level of complexity to what we see as well. But we may find that this is going to help us get the right things done inside of our coding

These objects are going to be useful because they will stay inside any of the various classes that you create. You will be able to look at these classes simply as the containers that are able to hold onto the information that is found in your objects or to organize the objects that you have. you want to make sure though that when you place some objects into a newly created class that you make, that these objects are going to have some kind of similarities with each other, and that they make sense for being in the same class.

This doesn't mean that we are going to have to have only identical objects together in order to make this happen. But if you find that someone else looks into one of your classes, you will find that they can look at the code and will have a good idea of why you grouped together all of the objects that are inside of that particular class.

An example that we are going to be able to see with this is a class that you created for dogs. You do not have to just add in St Bernard's or just one type of dog to that class. You are able to include big dogs, small dogs, and any kind of dog in between. Any dog that you are able to think about or gather up can be added to this class about dogs. Other programmers are going to be able to see that these objects are not identical to one another, but they will understand that these are all dogs, so they belong in the same class as one another.

These objects and classes are going to be able to work with one another because they can help to make sure that your Python code stays as organized as you possibly can. You can spend some time learning how to put these objects in with the right class along the way, and we can look at some of the codes to help with this along the way. even as a beginner, you will be able to notice how much easier this coding can be when you work on these classes and objects.

Some of the Features of OOP Languages

The nice thing about working with the Python language is that it is considered an OOP language. And this will allow you the option to include a lot of the features and more that these kinds of languages will provide to us. The OOP language is going to rely on the objects and their classes to get this to work. But there are also going to be some other techniques and structures that are associated with the objects that are supported in Python. These are going to be important to help us learn more about and can help us to see how these languages will work. Some of the features that we can enjoy when it comes to the OOP language will include the following:

Shared features from non-OOP languages: These languages may still have some features of low-level features from some of the older coding languages. Some of the examples of the features that are often still available in OOP languages include: Variables: These variables are able to store your formatted information inside a few different data types. These are built-in to your languages, such as integers and characters. Variables can include things like hash tables, string, and lists.

Procedures: These can go by different names such as subroutines, routines, functions, and methods. They are going to take your input and then generate an output that you can then use for manipulating your data. The newer languages will have more structured concepts like loops and conditionals, which are both used a lot in Python.

Classes and objects: We already spent some time talking about these through this chapter and will bring them up again later on. The classes are simply the containers that are able to hold onto your objects, no matter what kind of object you are working with. This helps you to call up those objects, or parts of the code, later on when needed.

Dynamic dispatch and message passing: As you write some of your own codes, you will find that the external code is not the one that is responsible for selecting the procedural code that the method call will execute. This kind of responsibility is going to the object. The object will do this by looking at the method that is associated with that object during run time in a process that is known as dynamic dispatch. It helps to make sure that all parts of the code work well together and that you don't run into any issues.

Encapsulation: This is a great feature that comes with the OOP languages. This is going to be a process that is going to help us to bind some of the data that we have. Any of the functions that we will see used for this process are going to be brought in to help manipulate the data and can help us to secure it from being misused in this code.

With the process that comes with encapsulation, we will get the benefit of knowing that when we call up the code, some other part is not going to be able to grab onto the code and make it go wrong. This will be one of the best ways to make sure that we are able to keep all of the objects in their right classes and to make sure that issues are avoided later on.

Inheritances: We are going to take a look at how some of these inheritances are going to work a little bit later on. But any of the objects that you have should be able to hold, at a minimum one, but often more objects inside of them. When this does happen, we are going to call it the process of object composition. OOP languages are going to also be able to support a process known as inheritances, which means that we are able to create a new part of the code with the features and more that comes with the parent code from before.

Open recursion: Along with some of the features that are found above with the OOP languages, you may find that some languages are going to support the open recursion option. This is where we are able to call over the object method and place it over to another method. You will just need to make sure that you use the keywords of self and this in order to get the process going. These variables are going to be known as late-bound, which means that they are going to allow the method that is defined in a class to invoke that method and then define it later on with some of your subclasses.

Of course, these are just a few of the great features that you will be able to use when it is time to work with an OOP language. As you go through this guidebook, you will soon see that there are a ton of features that come with these OOP languages and can help you to make sure that you are getting more out of your coding experience.

Coding Your Own Classes

Now that we have had some time to talk about the different things that you can do with objects and classes, it is time for us to go through and learn a bit more about how we are able to create some of our own classes, and how to make this whole process work. When we are coding in Python, we will spend some more time working on creating your own classes because it is going to help keep the code organized and will ensure that nothing will get lost along the way.

To help us to make one of these classes, though, you need to use the right keywords before we name the class. You can name the class anything that you would like in this process; we just have to make sure that the name is going to show up right after the keyword and that it is something that you are actually able to remember and hold onto later on.

Once you have had some time to name the class, it is then time to name a subclass, which is going to be placed inside of the parenthesis to stick with the proper rules of programming. Make sure that when you are near the end of the first line when you do create a class, that you have added in the semicolon to finish this off. While this is not something that is technically needed with some of the newer versions of Python and you can work the code if you forget to work with this part, it is still something that you should get done.

Writing out a class is going to sound more complicated at this point than it seems, so let's stop here and look at a good example of how you would be able to write out all of this in Python. Then we are going to be able to dive into a discussion as to what all of these parts mean, and why we are going to work with all of this as well:

class Vehicle(object):
#constructor

```python
def_init_(self, steering, wheels, clutch, breaks, gears):
self._steering = steering
self._wheels = wheels
self._clutch = clutch
self._breaks =breaks
self._gears = gears
#destructor
def_del_(self):
print("This is destructor....")


#member functions or methods
def Display_Vehicle(self):
print('Steering:' , self._steering)
print('Wheels:', self._wheels)
print('Clutch:', self._clutch)
print('Breaks:', self._breaks)
print('Gears:', self._gears)
#instantiate a vehicle option
myGenericVehicle = Vehicle('Power Steering', 4, 'Super Clutch', 'Disk Breaks', 5)


myGenericVehicle.Display_Vehicle()
```

If you would like, you can try out this code. Just open up your text editor and type the code inside. As you work on writing this out, you will notice that a few of the topics we have already discussed in this guidebook show up in this code. Once you have a chance to write out and then execute this code, let's divide it up and see what happened above.

One of the first things that we need to take a look at here when we are trying to set up some of our classes is the class definition. This is going to be where you will need o to instantiate the object, and then you will be able to get the definition of the class. The reason that we want to work with this is that it will ensure that we are always picking out the right syntax that we want to work within the code.

This is something that we need to pay some special attention to because it is going to be where we tell the compiler what we would like to see it do. And it is able to highlight the commands that we think are the most important. If you would like to bring out a new definition of the class, you are able to work with the right functions, either the object_method) or the object_attribute.

Then we can move on to some of the special attributes here. These are going to be found in a lot of the codes that we want to work with, so they are important in helping us see results. These special attributes are going to be good because they can provide a programmer with some peace of mind because you can take the right steps to ensure that these special attributes are going to not get messed up and will be used in the proper manner.

When you look through some of the codings above, you will find that there are already a few examples of the special attributes that you are able to work with. Some of the other options that you are able to work with here will include the following:

__bases__: this is considered a tuple that contains any of the superclasses

__module__: this is where you are going to find the name of the module, and it will also hold your classes.

__name__: this will hold on to the class name.

__doc__: this is where you are going to find the reference string inside the document for your class.

__dict__: this is going to be the variable for the dict. Inside the class name.

The last thing that we are going to take a look at here is how to access members of the class hat we have created. We want to make sure that when we write out certain codes for our needs that the compiler and the text editor have a way to recognize the classes that we are creating. This is going to make it easier to execute the code in a proper manner.

Before we can make this happen, though, we have to make sure that the code is set up in the proper manner. As you go through with accessing the class, you will find that there are going to be a few methods that we are able to use to make this work. All of them are going to have their own special times when you will use them, and all of them are going to do their job well. But the number one method that a lot of programmers are going to focus on here because it is efficient and more is the accessor method.

To show us some of the ways that we are able to work with the accessor method, and to help us understand some of this and how it will work with a class that we already created we need to first take a look at some of the coding that is below:

```
class Cat(object)
        itsAge = None
        itsWeight = None
        itsName = None
        #set accessor function use to assign values to the fields
or member vars
        def setItsAge(self, itsAge):
        self.itsAge = itsAge

        def setItsWeight(self, itsWeight):
        self.itsWeight = itsWeight

        def setItsName(self, itsName):
        self.itsName =itsName
```

```
    #get accessor function use to return the values from a
field
    def getItsAge(self):
    return self.itsAge
    def getItsWeight(self):
    return self.itsWeight

    def getItsName(self):
    return self.itsName

objFrisky = Cat()
objFrisky.setItsAge(5)
objFrisky.setItsWeight(10)
objFrisky.setItsName("Frisky")
print("Cats Name is:", objFrisky.getItsname())
print("Its age is:", objFrisky.getItsAge())
print("Its weight is:", objFrisky.getItsName())
```

Before we move on, type this into your compiler. If you have your compiler run this, you are going to get some results that show up on the screen right away. This will include that the cat's name is Frisky (or you can change the name to something else if you want), that the age is 5, and that the weight is 10. This is the information that was put into the code, so the compiler is going to pull them up to give you the results that you want. You can take some time to add different options into the code and see how it changes over time.

There are a lot of times when you will find that classes are going to be easy to work with. These classes are going to be a good option to help us take care of some of the information we have and can make it easier to take care of the different objects that are going to show up in our code as well. Both the classes and the objects are things that we need to spend some of our time on here because they ensure that the code is going to be organized and that we are going to keep things set up the way that we would like along the way.

Chapter 5: Working with the Python Namespaces

Another option or topic that we need to spend some time on when it is time to work with the Python language is the idea of the namespace. Think about how many conflicts in names that happen all of the time in real life. When we think back to our lives in school, how many times were you in a class hat had two or more students that shared the same first name? If someone went into that class and asked for one of those students who had the same name, everyone would wonder which one they wanted because there are two people by the same name.

Now, usually, this could be solved with having the last name attached to the first name. this is another layer to the process that will ensure that we got ahold of the person who we wanted, even if they did share the same name with someone else. While it would be nice if this were not an issue, we can't assume that everyone in the world is going to give their child a different name.

All of this confusion and the process of being able to figure out the exact person we would like to bring up, and looking for other information outside of the first name could be avoided if we found a unique name for each person. This may not be such a big problem when you are working with a small class of about twenty students. However, it is going to be really hard to come up with a unique name when you are dealing with hundreds, and maybe even thousands, of people. And the issue becomes even harder when we are talking about the whole world.

Another issue in providing each child in the world with a unique name is that we have to work with the process of determining if someone else also has their name, but used a different spelling. We could have a Macey, Macie, Maci, and Macy. These are all the same names, but they look unique, and it can be really hard to make sure that we keep it organized and more.

Then there is a similar kind of conflict that we are going to see when we are working with programming. When you are going through and writing out a program that is small, such as one that just has 30 lines and no dependencies outside of the program, it is pretty easy for us to go through and provide it with some meaningful and unique names for all of the variables.

But the same kinds of issues are going to happen when the code gets longer. When there are thousands of lines of code found in your program, and you add in some of the external modules that you need, this is going to become even more complicated along the way. and this is why we will find that working with namespaces is going to be one of the best options to work with.

What are These Namespaces?

So, to dive into this a bit more, we need to learn more about what a namespace is all about. This is basically going to be a system that will make sure that all of the names found in a program are unique and that we are able to use these without any conflicts along the way. you might already know that a lot of the things that show up in Python, such as the functions, lists, and strings, will be an object. Another thing that is interesting here is that Python is going to implement these namespaces as a dictionary.

There is going to be a process that is known as name to object mapping, with the names as the keys and the objects more as the values. There is the possibility to work with multiple namespaces, and this means that we are able to use the same name and map it to a different object. There are a few examples that come with these namespaces including:

Local namespace: This is going to be a namespace of local names that are inside of the function. This namespace is created when a function is called, and it is only going to last until the function returns.

Global namespace: This namespace includes names from a lot of modules that are imported that you will use with your project. It is going to be created when we have a module created in our project, and it is going to last until the script is able to end.

Built-in namespace: This namespace is going to including the function and exception names that are built-in to our code.

What is the Scope?

The namespaces are going to help us out a lot with this because it is going to uniquely identify the names that are going to be showing up in our program. However, this isn't going to imply that we are allowed to work with the name of a variable anywhere that we would like. A name also is going to come with a scope that is able to define the program parts where you are able to work with the name, without having to add in any of the prefixes that we think need to be there.

Just like what we are going to see with the namespaces above, there is the potential for multiple scopes to show up in the program. Some of the options that you will have when it comes to scopes that are available when you execute a program will include:

A local scope. This one is going to be considered the innermost scope that is going to contain a list of all the local names that we are able to use in our current function.

A scope that is for all of the enclosing functions. The search for a name is going to be able to start, in this situation, from the nearest enclosing scope and then will move out.

A module-level scope. This is going to be the one that will contain all of the global names from the module that we are currently in.

The outermost scope is also important here because it is going to be the one that will contain a list of all the names that are built-in. This scope is going to be searched last in order to find the name that you referenced at the time.

Working with the namespaces and more in the proper manner is going to be important when it comes to working with this kind of process it will ensure that your code is going to work in the manner that you would like and that when you call up a variable or another part of the code, it is going to work in the manner that you would like and that the code is going to behave and know what you would like to have to pull up. It may not seem like it is that important to learn, but it can definitely make a difference in the kinds of codes that you are going to write along the way.

Chapter 6: The Decision Control Statements

It is also possible to spend some time working with what is known as decision control statements. These are going to be important in helping you take some of the codes that you have and turn them into something that is going to be strong and will accomplish the work that you want. Plus, they will be able to help the compiler make some good decisions, without having to worry about whether you can guess all of the answers that are there or not.

As a programmer, it would be nice to come up with a guess ahead of time of what the user is going to add to the computer or the program ahead of time. but this is pretty much impossible. This is where the conditional statements are going to come in because they will make it easier to run the program in the manner that you would like. You can set up some conditions, and the compiler is able to use the conditions, along with the information that the user puts into the computer, in order to set things up as well.

You will find that these kinds of conditional statements are going to work with quite a few of the programs that you want to go through and write through this process. They are pretty simple, and it is possible to add more and more to them as you would need. And there are three main types that we are going to spend our time on, based on what we would like to see happen in the code. With this in mind, we are going to take a look at how to work with the if statement, the if else statement, and the elif statement to see how these are able to work for some of our needs as well.

Decision Control Statement # 1: The If Statement

First, we need to take a look at the if statement. This is the most basic of the three and can give us something to work off when we start to do the other two statements. The if statement is the most basic of these and will only let the program you write proceed forward if the answer provides it with the right answer. If the user puts in an answer, and the program determines that the answer is false based on the conditions that you set, then nothing will happen. If the answer is deemed true based on your set conditions, then the program will display some message or do another task you assigned to it.

You can probably already guess that this will cause some problems with most codes, but it is still important to know how to use these statements. A simple code that you can work with for these conditional statements include:

```
age = int(input("Enter your age:"))
if (age <=18):
        print("You are not eligible for voting, try next election!")
print("Program ends")
```

Now, when you work with this kind of conditional statement, there are a number of things that are going to show up with this kind of code. If you have a user who is on your website or using his program, and they state that they are under the age of 18, then the program, as it is written, is going to work just fine, and the message that we have there is going to show up. The user will be able to read that message before the program either ends or goes on to the next part that we have.

We can already see where this is going to cause a few problems along the way. With this one, if the user puts in that their age is over 18, then it is not going to meet the conditions that you place into the compiler. This doesn't mean that their age can't be over 18, but with the if statement, we have not set it up to handle any answers that are above 18.

As we have written out the code right now, nothing is going to happen if the user puts in that their age is above 18. This is because we haven't set it up. Right now, until we change over to the if else statements, later on, the user is just going to end up with a blank screen if they do happen to say that their age is more than 18 when they use this program.

Decision Control Statement # 2: The If Else Statement

The if statements are good to practice within the coding, but there aren't many times in your program where that is going to work. You want to have something come up on the screen when the user puts in their age, regardless of what their age is. If you used the if statement in the example above, your user will end up with a blank screen and no idea what is going on if they say their age is above 18. That doesn't look very professional and won't help you to keep people looking at your program.

A better option to use is the if else statement. These statements will provide an output to the user, no matter what they provide as their input. With the example above, the user may get the previous message if they state their age is 16, but then the code would also have a response if the user says their age is 32. It will respond to any answer that it is given, helping the code to keep moving through the program and ensuring that nothing just stops.

With the voting example that we had above, you can implement the following code to make an if else statement:

```
age = int(input("Enter your age:"))
if (age <=18):
        print("You are not eligible for voting, try next election!")
else
        print("Congratulations! You are eligible to vote. Check out your local polling station to find out more information!)
print("Program ends")
```

when we are working with this kind of option, we will see that he else statement is added to the thing. This else statement is important because it is going to be able to come into this program and will handle all of the ages that the user can input that are above 18. This way, if you have a user who is older than 18, they will be able to add on this age, and the program is still going to work the way that you would like.

You are also able to go through and add in a few more layers to all of this if you would like. For example, it is also possible for us to go through and divide it up so that we end up with four or five age groups, and each one will end up with a different kind of response in the process as well. And then you would add in the else in order to really catch all of the extras that are left that you did not think about ahead of time.

A good example of how this one is going to work is if you grab the code syntax above and then use it to ask the user what color is their favorite. You could then work with the if statements to help cover up some of the most basic of colors, such as black, orange, green, blue, red, yellow, and purples. If the user picks one of these as the color that they like the most, then the statement that you put with it is going to show up.

The else statement is going to be there because it is impossible to guess what answers the user is going to give all of the time. There are just too many colors out there, and so many of them have different names based on how you would like to use them. You can use the else statement is going to be there to help us catch any of the other colors that the user may choose as their favorite including white or pink or something else similar.

Decision Control Statement # 3: The Elif Statement

You can also look at using the elif statements in your code. The elif statements add on another level, but they are still pretty easy to work with. You can add as many of these into your code as you want, and then we add in an else statement to cover any other decisions that need to be taken care of in your code. Think of the elif statement like the old games where the user could pick from a menu the options that they wanted. This is similar to how the elif statement is going to work.

You can have as few or as many options as you want with the elif statement. You can choose to add in just two or three, or you could expand this out to twenty or more. The fewer options you have, though, the easier it is to write out the code that you want to use. A good example of a program that uses the elif statement is the following:

Print("Let's enjoy a Pizza! Ok, let's go inside Pizzahut!")
print("Waiter, Please select Pizza of your choice from the menu")
pizzachoice = int(input("Please enter your choice of Pizza:"))

```
if pizzachoice == 1:
    print('I want to enjoy a pizza napoletana')
elif pizzachoice == 2:
    print('I want to enjoy a pizza rustica')
elif pizzachoice == 3:
    print('I want to enjoy a pizza capricciosa')
else:
    print("Sorry, I do not want any of the listed pizza's,
please bring a Coca Cola for me.")
```

When we are working with this kind of code, you can see that the user is going to get a kind of menu of choices to show up, and they are able to go through and choose the type of pizza that they want to have in the game. But you are able to go through and change up this syntax so that you have something else showing up in the code that you want to use. If the user in this one does go and push the number 2, then they will end up getting Pizza Rustica as their choice. But if they find that they do not like any of the choices that they are presented with, and they would like to just get a drink in the game, then they could click on that option and get a pop in the process

Of course, this is a simple version of what we are going to see with these elif statements, and it is a great way to ensure that you are able to give your user a set of choices to pick from. In some of the other options, you could allow the user to add in the choices that they want, but when we are working with the elif statement, they are going to either pick out the one that they want that the game has provided, or you will have them go with the default option will be the one that shows up.

This is a good option to work with when you would like to create one of your own games, and you would like to give the user some options to progress the game on. You can also use this for testing someone online, or when you are doing a program that you need to limit the choices that the user will be able to pick out from the code.

These are some of the best conditional statements that you are able to work with when it comes to working with the Python program. You are able to make this be set up in a manner so that it will only able accept the right answer, make it so that the user is going to add in any of the answers that you would like and something will still show up, or you are able to create a kind of menu list in order to help the user pick out something that they would like. No matter which of the conditional statements that you would like to work with, you will find that working with these is going to really help us to get the results that we want in any program that we are creating.

Chapter 7: How to Handle and Raise Your Own Exceptions

We have spent some time looking at a lot of great topics when it comes to working in the Python language. We have taken a look at how to create a few things like conditional statements and some of our own classes as well. We looked at some of the basics that will come with this kind of language and how it can work for our own needs as well. But now it is time for us to go through and really see how we can work with something that is going to be seen as a bit more complex but will ensure that we are able to work on some of the codes that we would like.

In this chapter, we are going to take some time in order to look at a process in Python language is going to be the exceptions. We will look at how these are going to work as we write some of the different codes that are there. As we are doing this, you may notice that the library for Python is going to raise some of these through the compiler on their own. But then there are some times when you will want to raise up your own exceptions to help you see the results that you would like based on the kind of program that we want to write.

As you go through this process, you will find that these various types of situations where these exceptions are going to show up, and often they will look just like the error messages that you may have seen on some of the programs that you have done in the past. If one of these shows up, you should take the time to read through it so that you can learn more about the exceptions and see how they are going to work for your needs.

Now there are already going to be some of these exceptions that are found automatically with the library of Python. If you work on these and try to code with these in there, or if the user goes with one of these and tries to put these into the code as well, then the compiler will recognize that these are not allowed and will bring up the exception against what you are doing.

Then there are times when the program that you are trying to make in particular is going to end up with an exception that you have to be careful about. Your compiler is not going to see this as an issue on their own, but you will be able to take some of the steps that are necessary in order to handle these and to make sure that the compiler is going to raise the exception that you need.

One of the common exceptions that the compiler is able to raise in your computer is when the user tries to divide anything by zero. The compiler is going to see that this is something that should not be done, and it is going to raise up an alert when it sees that this is happening at the time. in addition, if you are working to call one of the functions that you did before, and you misspell it when you want to save it or call it up, then this is going to raise up another exception that we need to work with.

Now, you will find that there are quite a few exceptions that we need to pay attention to when it is time to work in Python. And some of these are going to be found automatically in the library that you will use in Python. It is a good idea for you to take a look at these and learn to recognize so that you are able to use them later. Some of the exceptions that are the most common in the Python language include:

Finally—this is the action that you will want to use to perform cleanup actions, whether the exceptions occur or not.

Assert—this condition is going to trigger the exception inside of the code

Raise—the raise command is going to trigger an exception manually inside of the code.

Try/except—this is when you want to try out a block of code, and then it is recovered thanks to the exceptions that either you or the Python code raised.

Raising an Exception

You now have an idea of what an exception is and how they are used, it is time to learn how to write one of these exceptions and what to do if one does show up in your own code. If you are writing your own code and you notice that there is an issue that is going to come up, then the compiler will raise an exception. Often the issue is a simple one, but other times they will require some work from you. An example of raising an exception includes the following code:

```
x = 10
y = 10
result = x/y #trying to divide by zero
print(result)
```

The output that you are going to get when you try to get the interpreter to go through this code would be:

>>>

Traceback (most recent call last):

      File "D: \Python34\tt.py", line 3, in <module>

      result = x/y

ZeroDivisionError: division by zero

>>>

When we take a look at one of these examples, you will find that the program will need to bring up one of these exceptions because the user is trying to divide that chosen number by zero. Remember that earlier, we talked about how this is an exception that is important when it comes to Python. If you keep the code written out the way that we have above, then you will find that when the program executes, you could get stopped right here with this error message. The code is going to let the user know that there is a problem. But the message that comes with this one is going to make it really hard for the user to have any idea what they did wrong. We have kind of a long and mangled kind of message that doesn't make a lot of sense unless you have spent some time working in coding.

The good news here is that we are able to make some changes to the code that we have above in order to deal with this. We can change up the message that we see in the exception, so that the user will actually understand what is going on, and can make a difference in what they are adding in as their input at this time.

When we are looking at the example above, you will want to make sure that the message we are working with will give the user some information on why this exception is happening. You want to put in something that is not going to be a string of letters and numbers that are messy, and one that is a bit easier to understand and work with. A good example of how we are able to work with this kind of exception includes:

```
y = 0
result = 0
try:
        result = x/y
        print(result)
except ZeroDivisionError:
        print("You are trying to divide by zero.")
```

Take a look at the two codes above. The one that we just did looks a little bit similar to the one above it, but this one has a message inside. This message is going to show up when the user raises this particular exception. You won't get the string of letters and numbers that don't make sense, and with this one, the user will know exactly what has gone wrong and can fix that error.

How Can I Define My Own Exceptions?

In the previous examples that we have gone through, we had a chance to really work with some of the exceptions that are going to be found automatically in our coding. These are ones that the Python library is already going to recognize on its own and will not need us to go through some of the added parts to provide it to us. But then there are also going to be some times when we are able to write out some codes, and we will want to raise our own exceptions to make this work.

Right now, we have focused our attention on the exceptions that are found automatically in our Python library. These are great to use in a lot of the codes that we want to focus on, but you will find that there are going to be some times when we would like to raise up one of the exceptions that are unique just to the codes that we are writing out on our own. For example, if we would like to work on a code that is going to only let the user pick out certain numbers, you could set up the program so that there is going to be some kind of exception raised if they choose the wrong kinds of numbers.

Working with these kinds of exceptions can show up in many of the codes that we would like to work with, and we will find that you may want to use them in games or some other kind of program. This is a popular option if you would like to just have the user guess three times at the game, or if you want to only give them so many choices to work with.

When we are working with these kinds of exceptions, you will find that you have to do a little bit of extra work because the compiler is not going to be set up to recognize that there is something wrong with the kind of answer that the user is giving to you. Technically, the user in your game should be able to go through and guess as many times as they want before the program moves on. But this can slow down the game and will make it more difficult for them when they don't know the answer and can't get the system to move on in the manner that it should.

These exceptions are going to be unique to your code, and without you writing them into the code as exceptions, the compiler would never recognize them as such. You can add in any kind of exception that you would like, and you can add in a message as well, similar to what we did above. The code that you will use to make this happen looks like the following:

```
class CustomException(Exception):
def_init_(self, value):
        self.parameter = value
```

```
def _str_(self):
        return repr(self.parameter)

try:
        raise CustomException("This is a CustomError!")
except CustomException as ex:
        print("Caught:", ex.parameter)
```

In this code, you have been successful in setting up your own exceptions, and whenever the user raises one of these exceptions, the message of "Caught: This is a CustomError!" is going to come up on the screen. This is the best way to show your users that you have added in a customer exception into the program, especially if this is just one that you personally created for this part of the code, and not one that the compiler is going to recognize on its own.

Just like we are able to see with the examples that we did at the beginning of this guidebook, we will see that we worked with just a bit of generic wording to show how the exception is going to work. But it is easy enough to go into the coding that we have above and then change it up so that you are going to get a unique message for the code that you are writing, and will ensure that the user is going to get a better explanation of what is going on at the time.

Working with exceptions is a great option when it is time to work with some of the codings that you would like to see within this language. You will find that as you progress through some of the different parts that come with this language, these exceptions are going to show up on a regular basis, and it will be helpful when you try to work with them later on.

There are many times that you will need to work with both types of these exceptions in some of the codes that you would like to work with, whether it is the ones that are found automatically in some of the codes that you are writing, or ones that you would like to raise up a bit in your own code. But knowing how to work with these will ensure that your program is going to work in the manner that you would like.

Chapter 8: Inheritances and How They Can Help You Reuse Code and Save Time

One of the neat things about spending some of your time working with a language that is considered an OOP language is that it allows us to work with a process that is known as an inheritance. These are great for enhancing some of the kids that you would like to write and can save us a lot of time. In fact, they can even allow users to write the code in a nicer and cleaner in the long run. These inheritances are going to be useful because you can take parts of the previous code you already wrote out, and reuse it in a new part. You can then go through and make some of the changes that you would like, keeping certain parts, deleting others, and making something brand new, without affecting the original part of the code as well.

Basically, when you want to work with one of these inheritances, you will find that you are able to take some of your original code, which is going to be known as the base code or the parent code. Then you are able to change up the parts that you would like to create the child code or the derived code. The methods that you will use vary based on what you would like to see happen with some of this code, but overall, it is going to help make your code stronger, and saves a lot of time. Even as someone who is just getting started with the ideas of coding, you will find that this can save time because you can create these codes without having to rewrite all of the parts over and over again. For beginners and more advanced programmers alike, this is always good news.

During the inheritance, you take your original parent code and copy it over to another part of the program. This becomes the child code, one that you can make changes to as you wish, without it affecting the original parent code at all. Sometimes you just need to copy it down once, and other times you will need to do it many times, but the process is the same.

To help make more sense out of these inheritances, how they work, and how they can help to keep your code clean and tidy and save you time, let's take a look at an example of how they look in your code:

```
#Example of inheritance
#base class
class Student(object):
        def__init__(self, name, rollno):
        self.name = name
        self.rollno = rollno
#Graduate class inherits or derived from Student class
class GraduateStudent(Student):
        def__init__(self, name, rollno, graduate):
        Student__init__(self, name, rollno)
        self.graduate = graduate

def DisplayGraduateStudent(self):
        print"Student Name:", self.name)
        print("Student Rollno:", self.rollno)
        print("Study Group:", self.graduate)

#Post Graduate class inherits from Student class
class PostGraduate(Student):
        def__init__(self, name, rollno, postgrad):
        Student__init__(self, name, rollno)
```

```python
        self.postgrad = postgrad

    def DisplayPostGraduateStudent(self):
        print("Student Name:", self.name)
        print("Student Rollno:", self.rollno)
        print("Study Group:", self.postgrad)

#instantiate from Graduate and PostGraduate classes
        objGradStudent = GraduateStudent("Mainu", 1, "MS-Mathematics")
        objPostGradStudent = PostGraduate("Shainu", 2, "MS-CS")
        objPostGradStudent.DisplayPostGraduateStudent()
```

When you type this into your interpreter, you are going to get the results:

```
('Student Name:,' 'Mainu')
('Student Rollno:,' 1)
('Student Group:,' 'MSC-Mathematics')
('Student Name:,' 'Shainu')
('Student Rollno:,' 2)
('Student Group:,' 'MSC-CS')
```

Overriding the Base Class

Now that the previous section has allowed us some time to talk about these inheritances and even look at some of the examples that we are going to see when it comes to working with these, it is time to learn how you are able to override one of your base classes or the parent class. There may be some situations where you will work on a new derived class, and then you find that it is best if you are able to override some of the things that were being put into that base class.

This may sound confusing, but basically, it is going to mean that we are able to use this to take a look into the base or parent class, and then change it up a bit to help us work on the new child or derived class that we would like along the way. the child class is going to be able to use all of these new behaviors, coupled with some of the old ones that we saved with the derived class, to get the results that we want in that part of the code.

Of course, this is going to sound more complicated to work with as you start out with all of this, and you may find that you are a bit confused when you would like to use this. But there are times when you would work with this because it will allow us to choose and pick some of the parental features that you want to put inside of this derived class overall. You can also decide which ones you would use later on, and which features are no longer necessary for this part of the class. Overall, this process is important because it allows us to make some of the changes that we want to some of the new classes we make, while always keeping the original parts of the base class that you would like.

The number of times that you would like to work with this, and how much you will be able to override in your code is often going to vary based on what that particular part of the code should be doing. You can keep it simple and work with some of the codings that we did above. Or it is possible to add in more steps and let this turn into something that is a bit more complicated. But no matter how you decide to work with these inheritances, they are useful at saving time, cutting out the clutter, and so much more.

There are many times when you will want to bring out the inheritance when it comes to your Python code. This allows you to take parts of the code from before, and then add in some of the new parts and take away the parts that you no longer want in order to create brand new parts of the code without as much work. This can make it easier to keep the code looking nice, and will save you time and hassle as we go through this process.

Chapter 9: Creating Your Own Loops in Python

The next thing on the list that we need to take some time to look at here is going to be the loops. These can be a lot of fun, and if we learn how to use them in the proper manner, they will help us to take many lines of codes, and cut them down into just a few lines instead. Loops are useful for cleaning up some of the code that we want to work with so that we can ensure a ton is able to show up in the code, without having to go through and write it all out.

For example, if you would like your code to be able to write out a big multiplication table, or list out all of the numbers in order from one to one hundred, you would not want to actually write out each of the individual lines of code to make this happen. This would take forever and look like such a mess, as well. But when you choose the right kind of loop for your needs, you will be able to get all of this done in just a few lines of code instead, and this will save you a lot of o time and hassle.

It is pretty amazing all of the information that we are able to add to a simple loop. We will take a look at a few examples of how these loops work later on, and describe the information that they are supposed to hold onto at the time. And you will be surprised at the amount of information that you will find stored in there. despite how much you are able to store in these, you will find that these are pretty easy to work with.

When the loops are set up in the proper manner, they are going to have the unique ability to tell the compiler how it should continue to read through the same line of code, over and over again, until a certain condition that you put in is going to be met. The manner that it uses to make this happen is going to depend on what kind of project you would like to work with, but you will find that it is going to work well.

For example, if you find that you would like to have the program write out all o the numbers that go from one to one hundred, then you would need to have the condition set so that when the code gets to any number higher than 100, which would be 101, then it will see that the condition is no longer being met and it will stop running the program.

One thing that we need to note at this point is that when we do work with these loops, we have to set the condition before we ever try to run or execute the code that we are working with. If you try to write out a loop that does not have this condition, then the loop has no idea when it should stop, and it will just keep going on and on and on. This effectively freezes up your computer and will mean that you have to stop the whole system to make sure that this works. This is why it is important that you double-check that the condition is there from the beginning to get the best results along the way.

As you work through creating some of the codes that are available in Python, you will find that there is actually more than one type of these loops that you are able to work with along the way. there are a lot of options that you are able to work with, but we are going to spend some time looking at the three options that you are most likely to use in the Python language. These are going to include the while loop, the for loop, and the nested loop. Let's get started with these.

The While Loop

The first type of loop that we are going to work on is the while loop. This loop is one that you can choose for your code when you know the specific number of times you want the code to cycle through that loop. You would use it to finish counting to ten for example. This one will need to have a condition, in the end, to make sure that it stops at the right point and doesn't keep going forever. It is also a good option if you want to ensure that your loop occurs at least one time before it moves on to the next part of the code. A good example of the while loop is the following code:

#calculation of simple interest. Ask the user to input the principal, rate of interest, number of years.

```
counter = 1
while(counter <= 3):
        principal = int(input("Enter the principal amount:"))
        numberofyeras = int(input("Enter the number of years:"))
        rateofinterest = float(input("Enter the rate of interest:"))
        simpleinterest = principal * numberofyears * rateofinterest/100
        print("Simple interest = %.2f" %simpleinterest)
        #increase the counter by 1
```

counter = counter + 1

print("You have calculated simple interest for 3 time!")

We need to take a moment to look through this kind of example. When this is being executed, you will find that it is going to allow the user to go through and add in any of the information that they would like that pertains to them, The code, when it has this information, is going to compute the interest rates for that based on the numbers that were put in.

For this particular type of code that we did above, we set it up so that the while, which is right at the beginning of the code that we have there, is going to be told that it should do the loop just three times. We can go through and make some changes to this and have it go through it more or fewer times if we would like. But for this one, we are allowed to put in three types of information and see the results, and then the loop will move on to something else in the process as well.

The For Loop

There are many times when we will want to spend some of our time working with the while loop. It can be a good one to spend some of our time on, and it is important for us to use it in some of the situations that we have. With that said, though, there are times when the while loop is just not going to work that well for our needs, and that is when we will want to bring in another type of loop that is going to be known as the for a loop.

In addition to spending some of our time working on the while loop that we discussed above, we may also want to spend some time with them for a loop. When you work with the loop, you will quickly notice that there are some differences, but it is still going to be useful, and it is something that other programmers are going to consider the traditional method for writing out the loops that they want to work with.

This is because there are just so many times when we are able to work with the for loop, and focusing on this and how we can make it work is going to be so important to some of the results that we are going to see along the way. in addition, we will find that we are able to use the loop for most of the situations where the while loop is useful as well. So, learning how to work with this one is often important, and if you are going to learn just one type of loop along the way, then the for loop is going to be the one that you would want to focus your attention on.

When you work with one of the for loops, your user will not go in and provide information to the code, and then the loops start. Rather, with the for loop, Python is set up to go through an iteration in the order that it shows up on the screen. There is no need for input from the user because it just continues through the iteration until the end occurs. An example of a code that shows how a for loop works is the following:

```
# Measure some strings:
words = ['apple,' 'mango,' 'banana,' 'orange']
for w in words:
print(w, len(w))
```

With this one, we can already see that the coding is a lot smaller than the other one, which is going to speed up the process a little bit and will make it slightly easier for you to work with. Take some time to open up the compiler that you are working with and type this one in. This will help us to get some more practice into what we are able to work within this kind of loop, and how it is different from the other two that we are spending our time on here.

The for loop, using the code that we are using above, is going to make sure that all of the words that are in the lines of code above are going to show up on our screen, but they will only show up in the order that you write them out inside of the code. If you do not like this order for some reason, you are not able to change it up when the code is executing along the way, but you can change it when you place them into the code to start with.

You can also go through this and make any changes that you would like to some of the codings that are above. You can add in some more words if you would like, add in some more information, and just make the loop look the way that you want. Just ensure that it is all in the right order before you try to execute it. Once the code is executed, you will not be able to make these changes later on.

The Nested Loop

And the third type of loop that you may want to use in your codes is the nested loop. Any time that you are creating a nested loop, you are taking one of the other loop type sand then placing it inside of another loop. Both of these loops are going to run at the same time, and both will continue until they are complete. There are many situations where you will want to work with a nested loop to help you get the code done. For example, if you want to create a multiplication table, the nested loop can be really nice to get this done. The code that you can use to get the nested loop to create a multiplication table is below:

#write a multiplication table from 1 to 10
For x in xrange(1, 11):
　　For y in xrange(1, 11):
　　Print '%d = %d' % (x, y, x*x)

When you got the output of this program, it is going to look similar to this:

1*1 = 1
1*2 = 2
1*3 = 3
1*4 = 4
All the way up to 1*10 = 2
Then it would move on to do the table by twos such as this:
2*1 =2
2*2 = 4

And so, on until you end up with 10*10 = 100 as your final spot in the sequence

You will notice with this one that any time that you would like to take one of the other loops, whether it is two of the for loops, two of the while loops, or one of each, and have them run inside of one another, then the nested loop is going to be one of the best options that you are able to use to make sure that this is going to get done in no time. You are able to combine together the parts that you would like, using the syntax from above, and get some great results in no time.

It may sound like something that is really complicated to work with, but you will find, and be able to see with some of the examples that are above, that it is actually an easy process to work with along the way. it will save up some of the space that you need inside of the code and can be done in just a few lines of code. Take a look back at some of the examples above and imagine how many lines of code it would take if you created one of these multiplication tables without using the loop.

As we explored a bit inside of this chapter, the for loop, the while loop, and also the nested loop are going to be some of the most common types of loops that work well in the Python language and that beginners are able to use when they are ready to write out some of their own codes in this language. You are able to use these codes to get a lot of work done in your program, without having to spend so much time writing out each line of code and hoping that it works the way that you would like. These loops can take potentially hundreds of lines of code and turn it around so that you are able to get it done in just a few, using some of the examples and methods that we talked about in this guidebook already.

Writing loops can make some of the more complicated aspects of writing code in Python easier than ever before. You will find that they are a lot easier to work with compared to some of the other methods that we may have discussed in this guidebook, such as the conditional statements, and you will find that it saves time while keeping the power that you need inside of some of the coding that you are writing along the way.

Chapter 10: The Python Variables

We can't end a discussion on the Python language without spending some time looking at the variables and what these are going to be able to do for some of the codes that we want to write out inside of this language. These variables are going to be easier to look at and work with than we may think in the beginning, but you will find that they do have a lot of power and are going to be so important when it comes to the coding that you will want to do here.

With that in mind, we need to take a look at what these variables are all about and why we need to work with them. To keep it simple, the variables are going to be anything in our code that is able to hold onto some value, especially one that has the potential to change. These are important for our coding because they will ensure that, when the code is running and needs the values, you will be able to pull these values out later and get them to work the way that you would like.

As you go through some of the codings that you plan to do with Python, you will find that these variables are going to be a good thing to learn how to use because they are basically reserving small spots of the memory of your computer. These spots are basically going to remain empty until you have gone through the process of assigning a value to them. But this spot is going to help us to keep the value we want in one place, and ensuring that the value will be called up at the right time.

The variables that you would like to create in this process are going to be found in different locations of the memory of any computer or system that you would like to use. The exact spot in the memory is going to depend on what you would like to see the code do and what kind of value, or values, you would like to assign to the variable as well. This is going to make it easier to find when you want to execute the code.

Depending on the type of data that we are working within this language, you will find that the variable is there to help us talk with the compiler. Basically, these will reserve some of the space that we need in the memory of our computer so that we are able to pull up that information later on and make it work for some of our needs. The compiler will know where that saved information on the computer is and can pull it out when it would like along the way too.

Another thing that we need to keep in mind before we learn how to assign a value over to our variable is that we can often put more than one value to each variable. In some of the first programs that you try to write out, you will most likely just assign one value to the variable that you have. but it is also possible that you will need to put two or more values to the same variable as well. If this is something that your program really needs you to work with, then this is definitely something that you can do. And it really doesn't take all that much work to accomplish. As we go through this chapter, you will see how this is possible and what steps you are able to take to make this work for your needs.

Assigning a Value to the Variable

Now that we have had a bit of time to talk about some of the variables that we want to work with, and some of the ways that they work to help out our programs, we need to look at the actual steps that we are going to take when it is time to assign a value, and sometimes more than one value, to the variable of our choice.

To make sure that the variable is doing what we would like, we need to make sure that the variable has at least one value that is assigned to it. This is an easy step to miss out on if you are hurrying through the program and not paying attention to what you are doing along the way. But if you do miss out on this step, then you are just going through and assigning an empty space in the memory, and nothing is going to show up in the code in the manner that you would like at a later time.

This is why we want to make sure that we are assigning some kind of value to the variable. If you have been able to add in the value over to the variable, and even if you add in more than one value to that chosen variable, then it will be able to pull this up later on, and you will get the code to react in the manner that you want in no time at all.

As you work with variables, you will find that there are actually three options that you can use. Each of them can be useful, and it will depend on the type of code you are working on and the value that you want to assign to that particular variable. The variables that you are able to pick from will include;

Float: this would include numbers like 3.14 and so on.

String: this is going to be like a statement where you could write out something like "Thank you for visiting my page!" or another similar phrase.

Whole number: this would be any of the other numbers that you would use that do not have a decimal point.

When you are working with variables in your code, you need to remember that you don't need to take the time to make a declaration to save up this spot in the memory. This is automatically going to happen once you assign a value over to the variable using the equal sign. If you want to check that this is going to happen, just look to see that you added that equal sign in, and everything is going to work.

Assigning a value over to your variable is pretty easy. Some examples of how you can do this in your code would include the following:

x = 12   *#this is an example of an integer assignment*
pi = 3.14   *#this is an example of a floating-point assignment*
customer name = John Doe   *#this is an example of a string assignment*

As we talked about earlier, though, there is another option that we are able to pull up here, and we need to take a look at how this is going to happen for our needs. This option is that we would take one variable, and assign two, and sometimes, even more, values to that same variable. There are going to be some of the codes that you want to write where you would need to have more than one value attached to the variable. The good news is that the process to get this done is easier to work on than you may think.

To make sure that we are able to get this done, though, we need to work with some of the same kinds of procedures that we did above. Just make sure that when we do this, we have an equal sign that goes to each of the parts that we would like to work with and that they attach the values back to the variable that we would like.

So, a good example of making this work is if we would write out a code that included something like the following $a = b = c = 1$. This one is going to show the compiler that all of these variables are going to equal one. Or you can write out something like $1 = b = 2$ to show that both the values of one and two are going to attach and belong to that variable.

One of the things that we need to remember here when we are working on this kind of coding, to ensure that the variables are going to behave in the manner that we would like to work with, is that the variable has to be assigned over to one of the values for it to work.

The variable on its own is just a spot that is reserved in the memory of our computer. Without a value assigned to it, though, we will find that it is not going to work the way that you would like at all. When you assign a value over to one of the variables that you have, you will find that when the code is executing, and the compiler calls up the variable, the right values are going to show up at the right times.

Chapter 11: Understanding the Operators and Where They Come Into Play

The next thing that we need to take a moment to look at in this guidebook is the idea of the operators. These are going to seem pretty simple to work with, but you will find that they are going to add in a lot of power to what you are doing in the code, and can really make a difference in the results that you are able to handle as well. Some of the different operators that you are able to work within the Python language will include:

The Arithmetic Operators

The first type of operators that we are able to spend some time on is going to be known as the arithmetic operators. If you are looking for something to help you get some more of your coding done, and add or subtract some parts of the code from each other, then it is important for us to learn how to use these operators. Basically, if you need to do any kind of math function in one of your codes, then you would want to work with this kind of operator to get it all done.

You are able to use any of the mathematical functions that you would like under this operator type. And you can add in as many of these as your code will need to get the work done. Just make sure that you work with the order of operations to help get this done and to ensure that it is going to match up in the manner that it should for your needs.

The Comparison Operators

There may be some situations where you are working on your codes, and you find that you need to compare more than one part of the code to another. Or maybe you need to take the input that the user is providing to you, and compare it over to something that you have inside your code, such as some of the conditions. There are many times when we are able to bring out the comparison operators, and learning how to make these work for some of our needs along the way will really help us to get things done and make sure that our conditions are met when the code works the way that we would like.

You will find that these comparison operators are going to be helpful when we want to write some of our codes because it allows us to take at least two, and sometimes more, parts of the code, whether it is the values or the statements, and then compare them with one another. When working on these, you may find that working with a Boolean expression is going to be helpful because it is going to give you an answer that will end up being true or false, which is pretty important when it comes to the comparison operators.

For example, if you are trying to figure out whether two parts of the code are comparable to one another, you would want to figure out if it is true that they are the same, or if it is false that they are not found as comparable, and these are examples of the Boolean expressions that you would like to work with. So, some of the statements will either be the same as one another or not. There are going to be some different operators that you are able to use with this and some of the options that you are able to choose to make this work include:

(>=): this one means to check if the left-hand operand is greater than or equal to the value of the one on the right.

(<=): this one means to check if the value of the left-hand operand is less than or equal to the one on the right.

(>): this one means to check whether the values of the left side are greater than the value on the right side of the code.

(<): this one means to check whether the values of the left side are less than the values that are on the right side.

(!=): this is not equal to the operator.

(==): this one is equal to the operator.

The Logical Operators

The third type of operator that we are going to spend some time on here is going to be the logical operators. These are not going to show up for us as often as we are used to seeing the comparison, the arithmetic, or the assignment operators, but you will still find that we need to spend some time on these and learn how they are going to work for some of our needs.

When we are talking about some of these logical operators, you will find that these are going to be used when we would like to be able to evaluate the input that our user provides to us, comparing them back to some of the conditions that we are trying to set in the code as well. Along with this idea, there are going to be three types of these kinds of operators that we are able to work with, and these are going to include:

Or: with this one, the compiler is going to evaluate x, and if it is false, it will then go over and evaluate y. If x ends up being true, the compiler is going to return the evaluation of x.

And: if x ends up being the one that is false, the compiler is going to evaluate it. If x ends up being true, it will move on and evaluate y.

Not: if ends up being false, the compiler is going to return True. But if x ends up being true, the program will return false.

The Assignment Operators

Then we are able to work with the assignment operators that are important as well. For the most part, we will find that we can use these operators to help us to assign a value over to the variable that we have. we have already taken some time to look at how these are going to save some space in the memory of our computer, and we need to make sure that we assign the value to the right variable. But we just have to make sure that we use the right symbol to make it happen.

The good news here is that the only assignment operator that we need to work with here is the equal sign. Put this right in between the value and the variable that we are working with to tell the compiler that these two go together inside of the code.

As we can see, there are a lot of great things that we are able to do when it comes to working with these operators. Making sure that they are set up in the right manner and that we use them properly is going to be important. Make sure to review these a bit and learn a bit more about how they are meant to work in order to see how powerful they can be for your needs.

Chapter 12: Working with Regular Expressions

The next topic that we are going to spend some of our time on is known as the regular expressions that are going to show up in the Python library. These expressions are going to be nice to work with, and when you decide it is time to work with these, you are able to continue with the same syntax on that expression, even if you need to go through and combine it with another language along the way.

So, if you are working with another code that would need to work with C#, C++, or Java to get things done, you would be able to use these regular expressions in order to make sure that you stick with Python. This is going to make it easier to add in some of the functionalities that you would like, even when another language needs to be introduced.

Any time that you would like to work with one of these regular expressions, you can head over to the library of Python and then take the expression from the library. You need to take some time to get this going right when you start working on this part of the program. Think about the library options that you would like to work with, import them in the beginning, and then they will be ready for you to go.

You will find that there are a number of options when it comes to the regular expressions that you are able to use in your code writing. Often these are going to show up with some of the statements that we are writing, and we have to make sure that the regular expressions are showing up in the proper manner. to help us make sure that these are going to work well, we need to first get a better understanding of how these expressions are going to work in the first place.

If you use these regular expressions in the wrong manner or you do not pick the right one, then the interpreter is going to have some trouble when it is time to read your commands, and you will not get the results that you want at the end of things. When you are ready to handle some of the work that comes with regular expressions to see what they are all about.

Some of the Basic Patterns to Use

Now that we have had some time to look a bit more at some of the regular expressions that we are able to work with when it is time to handle some of our work in Python, it is time to look at some of the basic patterns that are important in all of this as well. One thing that you are going to see pretty quickly when you are working with these kinds of expressions is that you will not just use them to pick out the fixed characters that you would like to use in the code. It is also possible for us to specify the patterns that could show up in our code. Some of the patterns that we will need in this kind of statement, as well as in other parts of our codes that need these regular expressions are going to include:

Ordinary characters. These are characters that will match themselves exactly. Be careful with using some of these because they do have special meanings inside of Python. The characters that you will need to watch out for include [], *, ^, $

The period—this is going to match any single except the new line symbol of '\n'

3. \w—this is the lowercase w that is going to match the "word" character. This can be a letter, a digit, or an underbar. Keep in

mind that this is the mnemonic and that it is going to match a single word character rather than the whole word.

\b—This is the boundary between a non-word and a word

\s—this is going to match a single white space character, including the form, form, tab, return, newline, and even space. If you do \S, you are talking about any character that is not a white space.

^ = start, $ = end—these are going to match to the end or the start of your string.

\t, \n, \r—these are going to stand for tab, newline, and return

\d—this is the decimal digit for all numbers between 0 and 9. Some of the older regex utilities will not support this so be careful when using it

\ --this is going to inhibit how special the character is. If you use this if you are uncertain about whether the character has some special meaning or not to ensure that it is treated just like another character.

As we can see here, there are a lot of different options that we are able to focus on when it comes to handling the basic patterns of these regular expressions. Some of these are going to be used more often than some of the others, but it is still important for us to learn how to use these and how to make these work for our needs. When we learn how to work with these, we will find that they are going to be good options to choose when you want to provide the compiler with the right instructions. Without these patterns in place, the compiler is not going to get the right instructions that you would like, and then the code will not behave in the manner that you would like.

How to Do a Query

The next thing that we need to spend just a few moments on in this chapter is the idea of how we can work with some of our regular expressions in order to complete a query for our needs. If we are looking to complete the process of doing a query, perhaps if we are working with Python to help us sort through and work with a database, then we would want to work with the idea of a query with the help of these regular expressions.

One of the things that we are able to do when we bring out these regular expressions is to work with a query. There are actually going to be several different methods that we are able to utilize to help us work on a query that we would like to see when investigating a string in the Python language. There are also a few methods that we are able to use in order to do these queries, and we are going to be able to take a look at these as well.

To help us before we get started on this, though, we need to take a look at the three methods. These are going to include the search, the match, and the findall methods to help us complete any of the queries that we would like. With these in mind, let's dive into each one to learn a bit more about how they work, and what we are able to do with each one to get our goals done.

Using the Search Method

When we are ready to work with our first method, which is the search method, we just need to make sure that we add in the function of search() into the syntax. This is going to be the function where we will be able to match up the right things in any location in the string. There will not be a lot of restrictions when it is time to find these right matches in the strings, as we see with a few of the other methods we will talk about. For example, there are going to be some options that will only allow you to look right at the beginning of the string to see if there is a match or not.

But when we take a look at the search method, you will be able to check whether or not there are matches that occur in the string. If there are no matches in that string, then you won't get a response at all. But if the program can find a match anywhere in the string, then you will get that returned to you. An example of how you would be able to use the search method, and what it would look like in your code is below:

import re
string = 'apple, orange, mango, orange'
match = re.search(r'orange', string)
print(match.group(0))

Using the Match Method

Along with what we are able to do with the search method, we can take this to the second step of working with the match method. This one is going to help us to look at the coding above in a slightly different manner. with this one, we will use the same code, but switch it out so that we end up with there. match rather than there.search part of the code. The match one though is going to just show us the matches if it is present at the beginning of the string that we are searching through.

So, when we take a look at the example that is above, we will find that the match method is not going to give us any results at all. Because apple is the word that shows up in the string and we are looking for orange, you are not going to get any results out of this at all. If you would like to check out whether the word orange is found in the code at all, then you would need to go back to the search method from before.

Using the Findall Method

And the final command that we need to take a look at when it comes to handling some of these regular expressions in this language is the findall method. This one is going to take a look at the string that we have and will release to us all of the times that a particular word is going to show up. So, if we want to figure out how many times oranges are listed in the code, then the findall method is going to be the one to use.

With the example that we did above in coding, if you did there.findall() method, you will find that you will get the word orange to show up two times because that is how many times it is found in the string. You can do this and get the results no matter how many of those items are found in the string. If we had listed out twenty oranges in the string, then this is how many oranges would show up on your screen with this one.

As we will see here, there are a lot of different options that we are able to work with when it comes to our codes, especially when we work with regular expressions. Each of these methods will make it a lot easier to find some of the information that you need, helps you to find out if there are some more patterns that are in the statements, and can make things easier overall.

Chapter 13: The Files of Python

When you are ready to write out some of the codes that you would like to do inside of the Python language, there may be some situations when you would like to take a lot of the data that you are already working with, and then learn how to store it, how to write it, how to create it and more. All of these are important when it comes to some of the files that we are able to work within this language, but learning how to do this is sometimes a little bit hard to work with.

If you are trying to save some of the coding and the data that you have to make it work for later, then you will find that saving it on a file on a disk, or working with it in the form on an inheritance like we talked about earlier, are two good methods to work with. This chapter though is going to take a look not only at how to handle the saving of files that we would like, but it is also going to help us to handle our files in other methods as well.

Before we dive into that too much though, we have to remember that there are going to be a few choices that we are able to make when it is time to work inside what is known as the file mode in this kind of language. To make this as easy to understand as possible, we can compare it back to how we work with a Windows file in Word. At some point when you are working with these files, you will stop and try to save that document that you are working with. But you can also modify that document and make some of the other changes that you would like.

The files that you are working with inside of Python will work in a manner that is similar. But rather than saving the pages of your document, you are going to take the steps that are necessary in order to save the codes that you are writing out as well. The good news here is that you are able to go through and work with a number of different operations when it comes to our codes. We are able to write out new code on a newly created file, seek out or move a file to the new location that we prefer, create a new file for our needs, and even how to close and save some of the codes that we have. Let's take a look at some of the steps that we are able to take in order to make this work for our needs.

How to Create Your Own Files

The first thing that we are going to explore when it comes to handling these files in Python is how to create a new file. This is a file that is responsible for holding onto a code that you would like to work with. If you would like to create one of your own files, and then write out some codes onto it, you first need to make sure that it is opened up and working in the IDLE.

While were are here though, we also get to choose which mode that we would like to focus on when it is time to write out some of the codes. The neat thing here is that you can choose between three different modes that will help you to go with the one that is going to work out the best for some of your needs. The three most common modes that work with creating your own Python files are going to include mode, append, and write.

Any time that you want to make some changes to the current file that is opened, you can use the (w) or write option because this is often the easiest one to work with. Any time that you are trying to open up a file and then write a new string in that file, you will work with binary files and will need the write() method. This is going to work well because it ensures that you will get the right characters returned at the end.

The write() function is really easy to use and allows you to make as many changes to the file as you would like. You can add some new information to the file, or you can make some changes to one that you opened up. If you are interested in doing the writing in the code, you can use this example to make things easier:

#file handling operations
#writing to a new file hello.txt
f = open('hello.txt', 'w', encoding = 'utf-8')
f.write("Hello Python Developers!")
f.write("Welcome to Python World")
f.flush()
f.close()

Now, before we take the time to move on from here, we need to open up the compiler that we have and write out the code. This is going to help us to get some of the practice that we need for later on and will ensure that we really learn how this code is going to work. This code, when it is written out properly, is going to help us to create a file and make sure that the information that is on that file will be in the right directory as needed.

The default directory where we are able to find all of this information and the file is going to be the one that you are currently in. you can go through and switch out the directory that is available and where you would like to store that information, but you will need to make sure that you change that over to be your current directory ahead of time, or you may not be able to find the information that you need later on.

Keep in mind with this one that no matter which directory you are in at the time that you are creating that new file, that is going to be the current directory. That means that you will need to move yourself over on the process in order to make sure that you are in the directory that you would like along the way as well. With the option above though, if you are in the current directory and you open it up, you are going to get the message that is there to show up on the screen.

At this point, you have written out the program, and there may be some times when you need to overwrite the program so that it will get a new statement to show up in a file that was already created. This is something that you can do with Python; you just need to change up the syntax that you are writing out. An example of how to do this includes the following:

#file handling operations
#writing to a new file hello.txt
f = open('hello.txt', 'w', encoding = 'utf-8')
f.write("Hello Python Developers!")
f.write("Welcome to Python World")

mylist = ["Apple", "Orange", "Banana"]

#writelines() is used to write multiple lines into the file

f.write(mylist)

f.flush()

f.close()

With the example that we just did above, you are able to see that we are really looking at how we are able to make some of the simple changes that are needed in order to see some good coding. Just by adding in a new line, we will be able to make things work the way that we would like. This example would not need to work with this line because it is simply adding in a few more words, but you are able to use this to your advantage in a lot of the codes that you are writing so keep it in mind when you are doing some of your files as well.

Handling the Binary Files

The second thing that we need to spend some time on here is how we are able to focus on some of the binary files that come with this language. This is a bit more complicated and maybe scary to work with, but basically, we are going to save this as an image file instead of the regular file inside of this language. It is actually easier to work with because you are able to take any of the data that you are working with or what to save, and then we can change it to an image or to a sound file, rather than having it be saved on the computer as a text file.

You are able to go through the process of changing out any of the coding text that you write in this language so that it becomes a binary file, regardless of whether it is a picture, sound, or text file to get started with. The thing that we really need to focus on and take into consideration when it comes to this though is that we have to supply the data inside of the object so that we are better able to expose this at a later time. The coding syntax that we are able to use for this one along the way is going to include:

```
# write binary data to a file
# writing the file hello.dat write binary mode
F = open('hello.dat', 'wb')
# writing as byte strings
f.write(b" I am writing data in binary file!/n")
f.write(b" Let's write another list/n")
f.close()
```

As we can see through this one, it is going to help us to make sure that we can take any of the other files that we have in Python, and change it over to a binary file. This helps us to save it a bit easier and will ensure that we are able to keep things organized.

Opening a New File

Now that we have spent some time taking a look at what we would like to see within our coding, such as how to create a new file and how to handle a binary file, it is time for us to move on to the third option that we are going to use when it comes to working with this kind of language. Opening up the file after we have had some time to save it, and you write it out before, then it is time for us to work with opening this up later to do some more work with it as time goes up.

When we take a look at the two examples that we have above, we already spent some time talking about how we are able to write out some words in our file, in one of the files that you created already, and you are able to change up the way that you save the file so that you can make it into a binary function that can come up later on. Now it is time for us to take a look at some of the coding that we are able to use here in order to ensure that we will be able to open up your file later on.

Once you have been able to open up that file, you will find that it is so much easier for you to work with it again and use it. Whether this includes making modifications to the code or messing around and adding some more parts of the code to this, it can all happen when you are ready to open up the file. Some of the coding that we are going to take a look at when it is time to bring out the codes that you would like to work with will include:

 # read binary data to a file
#writing the file hello.dat write append binary mode
with open("hello.dat", 'rb') as f:

```
        data = f.read()
        text = data.decode('utf-8'(
print(text)
```

the output that you would get form putting this into the system would be like the following:

Hello, world!

This is a demo using

This file contains three lines

Hello world

This is a demo using

This file contains three lines.

Seeking a File

And the final thing that we need to take a look at in order to ensure that we are going to be able to take care of ourselves and really make sure that we can find some of the documents that we need inside of this process, it is time to learn how to seek out a file.

Working with these files can be a good thing to learn when we are working in the world of Python coding. We have already taken the time to write out a new file, take a look at how to overwrite some of the data that we see in that file if we need, and we even took a look at how to open up the file. In addition to these, there are some times when we will find that the file is not in the right location, and we will want to make some changes to move that file to a new place.

For example, if you are doing some work on a file, and you find that things are not matching up in the manner that you would like, such as a misspelling of the identifier that we named, or you just find that the file is in the wrong directory, then it may be possible that you need to use the seek function to help you find that file, and maybe move it to the place that you would like.

As we work with this process, you will find that it is easy enough to go through and change up the position where the file is located so that it ends up in the right spot, or at least so that it will be a lot easier for you to find it. We just need to make sure that we are telling the code the right steps so that it knows where to put this.

And that is what we need to know when it comes to working with these files in the Python language. These files are going to help out in many situations when we are working with some of the codes that we would like to handle in this language. Make sure to take some time to try out these changes that you wrote, and so much more. This will help us to make sure that we know how to create a new file, make changes, and then get the files to work in the proper manner that we would like each time.

Chapter 14: Tips and Tricks to Learn More About Python

Now we are at the part of this guidebook where we need to take a look at some of the different tips and tricks that we need to focus on when it is time to write some of our own codes in the Python language. You will find that there are a lot of different parts that come with this kind of language, and learning how to make it work for our needs, and how to really get ahead of the game when we are learning something new, can be a challenge as well.

The tips and tricks that are in this chapter are meant to help you really learn how to work with some of the Python codings in the manner that you would like. This is going to make it so much easier for you to really write out some of the codes that you would like in this language. Some of the different tips and tricks that you can use as a beginner in coding in Python will include:

Do a Little Coding at a Time

The number one thing that we need to concentrate on here is doing just a bit of the coding that we want at a time. it is great news to go through and try to write out hours of code, but when it is time to run all of that code, later on, we will find that it is going to make things a little bit more difficult along the way.

Think about how many errors are going to show up, and all of the work that you will need to do to debug things and clean them up if you have to go through pages and pages of codes because you didn't stop and take a break.

It is often best if you just do a little bit of coding at a time. This will allow you a chance to focus on the coding that you would like to do, without having to worry about fixing all of those mistakes. If you just do a small block of coding, and then run it, if there is an error that is found int hat information, you will know exactly where the error is and can fix it in just a few moments rather than spending hours along the was as well.

You should also start out small with some of the codings that you are doing. You do not need to go through and spend hours on coding to get better. This is sometimes a daunting amount of time for someone who is just starting out and can make it so that some people will give up right at the beginning. You should consider just starting off with fifteen to twenty minutes, and then building up from there.

Along with this same idea, we want to make sure that we are taking breaks when they are needed. It is great that you are excited to get started with some of your work in coding and such. But if you jump right in and spend hours a day working on the coding, you are going to get worn out and tired in no time at all. This is not a good way to start out with coding at all and can take some of the fun out of the process as well.

Another issue that comes up here is that it is hard to take a break and stop doing the work when you are struggling with solving a problem. This is often going to be a hard thing to handle. We see that we are in trouble with a problem, and we want to be able to fix it before we give up. But sometimes, when we spend too much time on a problem, and we focus on it too much, we will find that it is going to just make things worse.

Our minds are tired, we forget what we have done in the past already, and it just gets more and more difficult to handle overtime as well. Learning how to just take a break, and walk away from the problem is going to be a big challenge in all of this. And often, once you do take this break, you will find that it is going to be a lot easier for you to really come back with a fresh mind, and without all of the frustration from before, and you can actually solve the issue faster and easier than before.

Do Some of the Practice Options

This guidebook took some time to show us a few of the practice options that are out there along the way for some of the work that you would like to do with your coding. This is a great place to get started to ensure that your code is going to work the way that you would like. In addition to this though, we need to spend some time getting as much practice as possible along the way.

The more times that you can practice the codes that we are learning, the better off you are going to be. Spend some time trying out the code in this guidebook, along with some of the other codes that are out there, and then figure out how you can make some changes and modify some of this stuff to ensure that it is going to work the way that you would like along the way.

You are never going to get better at some of the codings that you would like to do if you don't first take some time to practice. All of the good coders out there are going to have spent quite a bit of time practicing the codes that we want to work with, and you can get better along the way as well.

Print Out Things Along the Way

The more that you are able to go through and print out and execute the code that you are working with, the easier it will be to see what is going on along the way. if one block of code works well, then you will find that it is going to be easier to tell when something is wrong. You will be able to go back and see that something is wrong, and where that thing that was wrong is located, faster than before

Printing off a part of the code is a simple process that will help you to really see what is wrong, and will ensure that you are able to fix mistakes early on. If something brings up an error, or it doesn't work the way that it should, then you are able to go through and fix that part of the code. It is sometimes going to slow down what you are doing in some of the codings, but it is definitely going to make a difference and will help us to fix mistakes and errors quickly, without issues along the way.

Comment Out Your Code

If you find that you are not able to figure out what is wrong with your codes, then it may be a good option for you to comment out some of the code to see what will fix it and what doesn't seem to make a difference. You may find that sometimes commenting out the code that you write will ensure that you are actually able to find some of the mistakes and the errors that are there easier than before.

When you are dealing with some of the options that cause errors, and you are not able to find the issue. Maybe you have tried out a few different things, and it is just not working the way that you would like. When you comment things out, you can continue working on the code, and adding and taking things away, until you figure out the part that seems t be causing you the problem.

If you comment something out and it seems to solve the problem with the code that you are writing, then it is likely that you are going to end up with the solution to the problem. You will then be able to focus on that part of the code, making the necessary changes that you need and fixing it up. This process may be a bit slow and take some time, but it is better than just going in circles on this and will ensure that you will actually find the issue.

Practice Makes Perfect

The more that you are able to practice some of the coding that you are doing along the way, the better your own coding skills are going to get. You do not want to just try the codes in this guidebook once and then never do any work on coding again. This is not going to make you an expert. It may be a good way to get started, but you still have a lot of work to go before you are able to write out some of your own codes as well.

The first step is to go through and make sure that you really know how to work with some of the codes that are in this guidebook. These will help you to learn more about how these are going to work with these codes and gives you some of the basics that you need. Mess around with these a little bit to get the feel for them a bit more, and then figure out whether you can make some changes to ensure your codes work well.

But do not stop right here. You also want to try out new codes and more as you go along. The more practice that you are able to gather up and do each day, the better your coding skills are going to get. You may find that when you spend a bit of time coding and trying out some of the practice tests and games that are available online, that you are going to get this turned into something that is more fun and can help you to enhance your learning overall as well.

Ask for Help When Needed

Sometimes, you are going to need to ask someone else for some help when it is time to work with your coding in the Python language. It would be nice to be able to go through and write out the codes the right way all of the time and not have to ask anyone for help. But coding is complicated, and learning how to make this work for our needs is going to be important along the way, and sometimes that requires us to have someone around who can help us when we get stuck.

One thing to keep in mind while we are going through some of this coding, though, we should not just jump over and ask someone for help the moment that an error sign shows up. It would be nice to get help all that often, but it is not going to help you to learn how to code, and will basically just be the same thing as having someone else do the coding in the first place for you.

Rather than letting that happen, you will need to go through and consider whether you have done all of the troubleshooting that is needed along the way. You can try to find some of the error messages, go through and see how to debug the program, and more. Once you have tried out a few things and you are stuck at what is going to fix the issue, then you will need to consider asking someone to give you some advice and help.

When you do ask for help, try to be as efficient as possible. This will ensure that you will be able to avoid wasting the other person's time and will ensure that you are going to see the results that you would like faster. First, make sure that you let the other person know what you are hoping to get the code to do if it were working in the manner that you wanted. Then explain what seems to be going wrong in that part of the code and what you would like to get some help with.

Also, take some time here to explore what you have already been able to do. This shows the other person that is coming in to help you, that you have at least tried something, and can save time, so they don't go through and try the same things again. Make sure to check out what they are doing and ask questions as they do it. This information can be useful when you try to fix some of the issues in your code on your own later on.

Learn Some Common Error Messages

As a beginner, there are going to be times when your codes are not going to work the way that you would like. It would be nice in a perfect world to write out codes that worked each and every time. It would be nice for us to never have to worry about debugging the program or worry about an error message showing up when we write the codes. But this is not the reality.

Especially when you are first learning how to code and how to make things work in this process, we have to consider that there are going to be some kind of error message that will show up in some of the codes that we are trying to write out along the way. Knowing how to handle these errors and knowing what they mean is going to make a big difference in the results that you would like as well.

You will not be able to learn all of the error messages that you are most likely to need as a beginner. You can research some of these in order to figure out what you most likely need and then get these down so that, when they do show up in your code, you will recognize them and will know what changes you will need to make along the way as well. This will not cover all of the errors, but you will find that having a few of these down will make it a lot easier and can ensure that you will save time compared to just wondering what the error message is about ahead of time.

In addition, we have to consider that sometimes we will still not know what the error message is all about. This is why we may need to still do some research when these error messages come up. You will be able to do a Google search of some of these terms and errors and then see what is going to come up with that. If you are dealing with these errors it is likely that someone else has too. So, it is a good idea to look it up and see what information you are able to find as well.

Don't Be Scared to Try Something New

Yes, coding is going to be difficult to work with sometimes. This is why not everyone is going to come through in order to learn how to work with the coding that you would like. It is important for you to spend some time trying things out, and work with things that are brand new and that you do not know much about. This is the only way that you are able to learn something new and will be able to see the results that we need in coding in order to get that application and program done.

If something seems hard at first, take some time to experiment with it a little bit and learn how you can make it work for your needs. Break it down into smaller pieces so that you are able to work with it a bit more. If you just need to do one part at a time, then you will find that this is going to be a less complicated part, and will help us to get more done.

When you really want to work on a complicated piece of code, and you want to ensure that you are going to be able to get the most done out of your programs and applications, then you have to be willing to take a risk and see some good results as well. It may be hard, and it may be a little bit scary, but you will find that working with this approach is one of the best ways to make sure that you are set to go.

Print Off Some Cheat Sheets

One thing that we need to try out when it is time to work with some of the codings that we want to work with is to work with some cheat sheets. Remembering all of the different codes that we want to use is going to be hard. And some of these will be hard to remember because they are more complicated and harder to work with. These cheat sheets will make it easier for us to take a look over at some of the codes that we are trying to explore and work with, and will ensure that we are able to get some of the results that we want without having to search for them each time that we need them.

The internet is going to have a wealth of information that we are able to use when we would like. But you will find that searching around and trying to find the information that you would like is going to take some time and can be hard for us to handle sometimes. And it takes a lot of time. You will get frustrated and may decide to give up. These cheat sheets are going to be a lifesaver to help you to get things done and make it easier.

There are a lot of ways that you can make these cheat sheets work for your needs. You will find that you are able to go through and write them out if you would like, print them off with some larger print, and more. You have to choose the method that works the best for your needs in order to really see the results and to make your own coding easier overall.

There are a lot of great tips and tricks that we are able to work with when it comes to making sure that our codes will work out great in our Python language. Setting this up so that it works well, and that even some of the more complicated codes are going to work the way that you would like. Make sure to follow these techniques and more to ensure that you are going to see the results that you would like.

Conclusion

Thank you for making it through to the end of *Learn Python Programming*, let's hope it was informative and able to provide you with all of the tools you need to achieve your goals whatever they may be.

The next step is to spend some time taking a look at some of the different parts that we are able to focus on when it is time to work with coding our own applications and more. Many people are worried about getting into coding because they think that it is going to be too difficult for them to get started, and they worry that they will never be able to handle all of the work that is going to come with their coding needs.

And that is part of the beauty that is going to come with using the Python language, and we hope that you are able to see this when it comes with this kind of language and with the examples that are in this guidebook, you will find that you will be able to work with the Python language. This is going to be an easy language for beginners and advanced coders to work with, but you will find that it has a lot of power behind it and will help you to get some of the work done in coding that you would like.

This guidebook has spent some time looking at the benefits of working with the Python language, and all of the different options that you are able to work with when it comes time to work on your program. We spent some time looking at how to write out some of our own conditional statements, our loops, exceptions, inheritances, and so much more. We even spent some time looking more in-depth about the work we can do with OOP languages and the classes that we would like to work with, and this will ensure that we can keep things as organized as possible within the code that we do.

When we are able to put all of these parts together inside of our work of coding, you will find that it is a lot easier to work with some of the codings that we want, even when we are a beginner. You will find that this is easier to accomplish than you think, and we are able to make codes that work with all sorts of projects. And considering that Python is going to work well with a lot of the major companies out there and some of the platforms that they want to use as well, including the Google search engine and some of the functionality of the YouTube site, you can see why this is a language that you are able to learn, and get a lot of use out of as well.

You no longer have to be worried or scared about working with a coding language. While some of the coding languages in the past may have been a bit difficult to work with and would not provide you with the results that you wanted all of the time, you will find that Python is not going to come with this kind of situation at all. You may have even glanced through some of the different parts of this ahead of time and noticed that it is easy enough to read some of these codes, before even starting. Take that as a confidence boost, and see how easy working with this language can be.

There may be a lot of different coding languages that we are able to work with when it comes to focusing on the coding that you would like to accomplish. But Python keeps proving that it is one of the best options out there for us to work with. When you are ready to learn more about coding in Python and all of the neat things that we are able to do with it, make sure to check out this guidebook and take a look at how great it can be.

Finally, if you found this book useful in any way, a review on Amazon is always appreciated!

www.ingramcontent.com/pod-product-compliance
Lightning Source LLC
Chambersburg PA
CBHW071138050326
40690CB00008B/1496